JUAN PONCE DE LEÓN

Please visit our web site at: **www.worldalmanaclibrary.com**
For a free color catalog describing World Almanac® Library's list of high-quality books and multimedia programs, call 1-800-848-2928 (USA) or 1-800-387-3178 (Canada). World Almanac® Library's fax: (414) 332-3567.

Library of Congress Cataloging-in-Publication Data

Green, Tamara, 1945-
      Juan Ponce de León / by Tamara Green — North American ed.
          p. cm. — (Great explorers)
      Includes bibliographical references and index.
      Summary: A biography of the Spanish explorer who sought fruitlessly to discover a fountain of youth in Florida and the Caribbean.
      ISBN 0-8368-5018-1 (lib. bdg.)
      ISBN 0-8368-5178-1 (softcover)
      1. Ponce de León, Juan, 1460?-1521—Juvenile literature.   2. Explorers—America—Biography—Juvenile literature.   3. Explorers—Spain—Biography—Juvenile literature.
4. America—Discovery and exploration—Spanish—Juvenile literature.   [1. Ponce de León, Juan, 1460?-1521.   2. Explorers.   3. America—Discovery and exploration—Spanish.]   I. Title.
II. Great explorers (Milwaukee, Wis.)
      E125.P7G74   2001
      975.9'01'092—dc21
      [B]   2001026812

This North American edition first published in 2002 by
World Almanac® Library
330 West Olive Street, Suite 100
Milwaukee, Wisconsin 53212 USA

This U.S. edition © 2002 by World Almanac® Library.
Created with original © 2001 by Quartz Editions,
112 Station Road, Edgware HA8 7AQ, U.K.
Additional end matter © 2002 by World Almanac® Library.

Series Editor: Tamara Green
World Almanac® Library editor and contributing writer: Fiona Macdonald
World Almanac® Library project editor: Betsy Rasmussen
World Almanac® Library designer: Melissa Valuch

The creators and publishers of this volume wish to thank the following for their kind permission to feature illustration material: Front cover: main image, Helen Jones/ other images Bridgeman Art Library/ AKG/ Tony Stone Images/ Natural History Photographic Agency/ The Art Archive; Back cover: AKG/ Bridgeman Art Library/ The Art Archive; 5 Tony Stone Images; 6 Bridgeman Art Library; 7 Helen Jones; 8 t Bridgeman Art Library/ b Tony Stone Images; 10 Robert Harding Picture Library; 11 Mary Evans Picture Library; 12-13 Stuart Brendon; 14/ t The Art Archive / b Bridgeman Art Library; 16 t AKG/ b Bridgeman Art Library; 17 Bridgeman Art Library; 18 Bridgeman Art Library; 19 AKG; 20 Bridgeman Art Library; 21 AKG; 22 The Art Archive; 23 AKG/ b Mary Evans Picture Library; 24 t AKG/ c The Art Archive/ b Mary Evans Picture Library; 25 Bridgeman Art Library; 26 t Mary Evans Picture Library/ b The Art Archive; 27 Bridgeman Art Library; 28 Tony Stone Images; 30 Bridgeman Art Library; 32 t Bridgeman Art Library/ b AKG; 34 t Natural History Photographic Agency/ b AKG; 35 t AK /b Robert Harding Picture Library; 36 t Tony Stone Images/ c Bridgeman Art Library/ b Ancient Art & Architecture Collection; 38 AKG; 39 AKG; 40 t The Art Archive/ b Bridgeman Art Library; 42 t AKG/ b Bridgeman Art Library; 43 Helen Jones

Printed in the United States of America

1 2 3 4 5 6 7 8 9 06 05 04 03 02

JUAN
PONCE DE LEÓN

TAMARA GREEN

WORLD ALMANAC® LIBRARY

CONTENTS

INTRODUCTION

**JUAN PONCE DE LEÓN explored the
Carribean region of the Americas.
He reported on the importance of the
Gulf Stream, as well as giving
Florida its name.**

Juan Ponce de León and his crew sailed past numerous small islands (*above*) on their approach to the coast of Florida.

Ponce de León had set out from Puerto Rico when he first came upon Florida. A corner of Puerto Rico's present-day capital city San Juan is shown here (*below*).

Juan Ponce de León was born into a noble family in a region of northern Spain. In 1493, he traveled with Christopher Columbus on the second of that explorer's voyages to the Americas. For the next 28 years, Ponce de León explored the Carribean, collecting wealth and information for the kings and queens of Spain.

His close contact with various Native American peoples allowed Ponce de León to learn about and appreciate cultures and traditions different from his own. It also allowed him to hear local stories and legends, including one about magical waters that could restore youth. The king of Spain encouraged Ponce de León to locate this Fountain of Youth. During this search, Ponce de León saw and named Florida.

Although Ponce de León failed to find the Fountain of Youth, he succeeded in observing and reporting on the Gulf Stream, an important natural feature that has a tremendous impact on shipping.

JUAN PONCE DE LEÓN

SOLDIER AND EXPLORER

This detail (*above*) is part of a plan of Cádiz (in Spain), from where Ponce de León sailed with Columbus in 1493.

Spanish explorer Juan Ponce de León is remembered as one of the first Europeans ever to set foot on mainland America. He also gave Florida its name.

Juan Ponce de León was born in the village of Santervás de Campos, in the province of Valladolid in northern Spain. The year of his birth was probably 1474, but a few historians have suggested the earlier date of 1460. His parents came from respected noble families but did not have money, land, or power. They died young, so Juan Ponce de León and his brothers had to make their own way in the world. His older brother married a rich heiress, and his younger brother became a Roman Catholic friar. Juan himself found work as a page in the household of a distant relative, Don Pedro Nuñez de Guzman.

Don Pedro was a close friend of the Spanish royal family and a tutor to one of the king's sons. Like all nobility at that time, Don Pedro employed many servants. In return for running errands and waiting tables, Juan and the other page boys received food and lodging and were taught reading, writing, polite speech, and good manners.

When he was about 14 years old, Juan Ponce de León became Don Pedro's *squire*, or "personal assistant." His most important task as a squire was to help his master get ready for war by cleaning and checking his weapons and

An artist's conception of a Spanish explorer on horseback riding through the forest on an island in the Caribbean (*left*).

> **"** *A valiant military man, skillful leader, loyal subject, honest administrator, loving father, and hard-working colonist.* **"**
>
> WORDING ON PONCE DE LEÓN'S TOMB

armor and escorting him to the battlefield. He was given training in horseback riding, sword handling, and spear handling so that he could help his master fight.

WHAT'S IN A NAME?

The name Juan is the Spanish version of John. Juan Ponce de León's father's family name was Ponce. De León was later added so that everyone would know that the Ponce family had once been important in León, a region of Spain where some of his relatives still owned property, including an island called León. The city of Cádiz was built on León and was one of the best harbors in Europe and the main port of western Spain. Juan would have pronounced his name "Hwan PON-thay day Lay-ON," and that is how speakers of Spanish in Europe still say it.

No European country known as Spain yet existed when Ponce de León (*right*) was born in 1474. He came from Castile, one of several kingdoms in that part of the world.

A detail from a 16th-century engraving depicting a European artist's conception of Native Caribbean people (*below*).

Ponce de León left his home on Hispaniola for San Juan Bautista (known as Borinquén to its Native population). It was a bold step at the time, because the island was still uncharted. It was not long, however, before Ponce de León was appointed as governor. Today, the island is known as Puerto Rico, and its capital city of San Juan is shown here (*below*).

A DIVIDED LAND

At the time Juan Ponce de León was born, Spain was divided into two separate states, Aragón and Castile. From 1479, the two states were ruled jointly by Ferdinand, the King of Aragón, and Isabella, the Queen of Castile, who were married to each other. Later, in 1516, Aragón and Castile were united to form the kingdom of Spain, which still exists today.

Ferdinand and Isabella shared many political ambitions. In particular, they wanted to conquer more overseas lands than their neighbor and rival, Portugal. They also wanted to force all non-Spanish people out of Spain.

Since the 8th century, southern Spain had been home to a Muslim civilization based in the cities of Córdoba and Granada. Muslim merchants, artists, craftworkers, doctors, scientists, and scholars had come from North Africa and the Middle East to settle in Spain. Many respected and successful Jewish men and women also lived there. Muslims, Jews, and Christians all lived and worked together in peace and harmony even though the kings and queens of Aragón and Castile regularly tried to take over the land that the Muslims ruled.

TWO FIERCE WARS

From 1475 to 1479, Ferdinand and Isabella sent Spanish soldiers to fight against Portugal. After that, they decided to declare a fresh *crusade*, or "holy war," against the Muslim rulers of southern Spain. Their armies attacked all non-Christians living there. Ferdinand and Isabella also called on the Roman Catholic Church to set up an inquisition, which is a religious court that had the power to imprison and torture anyone who refused to accept Catholic beliefs. Faced by this double attack, Muslims and Jews fled in terror. By 1492, they had all left Spain.

DID YOU KNOW?

Few documents or other kinds of evidence survive to tell us about Ponce de León's early life. Some writers in the past claimed that he fought in Spain's war against Portugal (1475-1479), but if Ponce de León was born in 1474, he would only have been five years old at the time.

A YOUNG SOLDIER

Juan Ponce de León took part in the war against the Muslim cities in Spain. At first, he helped his master and other experienced fighters. He quickly proved himself strong, brave, and quick-witted enough to become an independent foot soldier, fighting alongside experienced soldiers when he was just 18 years old.

A GOOD MOVE

When the war ended in 1492, Ponce de León had no work to do. At that time, Spanish kings and queens had no full-time armies. Soldiers were paid while they were fighting but were expected to find other work in times of peace. In 1493, Ponce de León decided to visit the port of Cádiz. No one knows why — perhaps he hoped to find a job there, or maybe he planned to ask his wealthy relatives on the island of León for help. Whatever the reason for his visit, it changed his life.

At Cádiz, Ponce de León met famous Italian explorer Christopher Columbus. In 1492, Columbus had made a historic voyage across the Atlantic Ocean from Spain to the Bahamas and the islands of the Caribbean Sea. He had returned to Spain early in 1493. Now he was assembling a fleet of 17 ships in preparation for a second transatlantic voyage. This was a tremendous opportunity for adventure and a chance to gain wealth and fame. Although he had no experience as a sailor, Ponce de León persuaded Columbus to let him join the crew.

> " *Captain in Española, governor in Borinquén, and discoverer and first governor of Florida.* "
>
> WORDING ON
> PONCE DE LEÓN'S TOMB

TIME LINE

1474
Ponce de León's probable date of birth (or 1460).

1492
Ponce de León is unemployed after Spain's war against Muslims ends.

1493
Ponce de León sails to the Caribbean with Columbus.

1504-1505
Ponce de León takes part in the conquest of Hispaniola. He is rewarded with land and becomes the first governor there.

1505
Ponce de León founds a new town in Higüey and names it Salvaleón.

1506
Ponce de León makes his first visit to Puerto Rico.

1509
Ponce de León becomes governor of Puerto Rico.

1513
Ponce de León lands on and names Florida. He notices the Gulf Stream.

1514
Ponce de León is knighted by King Ferdinand.

1521
Ponce de León dies in Cuba.

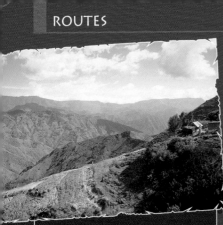

Two recent photographs of the island of Hispaniola in the Caribbean. One depicts a view of the interior (*above*); the other shows the coast (*below*).

A NEW WORLD

Ponce de León lived at a time when European sailors were making daring voyages across oceans to explore lands in Africa, Asia, and the Americas.

Spain and its neighbor Portugal are the most westerly countries in continental Europe. Both have coastlines bordering the Atlantic Ocean and a long tradition of seafaring. By the 15th century, Spanish and Portuguese sailors were becoming very curious about what lay beyond the European seas they knew so well. Encouraged by enterprising rulers such as Prince Henry the

Navigator, who lived from 1394 to 1460, sailors from Portugal had set out on voyages south to explore the African coast. By 1498, they had rounded the southern tip of Africa and reached Goa in India.

Spanish and Portuguese explorers had also sailed west into the high waves and strong winds of the Atlantic Ocean, and some settled on remote islands off the coast of Africa, including the Canary Islands and the Azores.

Castilians built the first cathedral in the New World in what is now the Dominican Republic, a part of the island of Hispaniola. Hundreds of years later, it is still standing, as shown in this photograph (*left*).

MAKING HEADWAY

Elsewhere in Europe, adventurous scholars, merchants, soldiers, and missionaries also planned journeys to faraway lands, by both land and sea. They hoped to gain knowledge, make fortunes, conquer empires, or convert others to their faith. They especially wanted to find new routes to the rich lands of India, China, and Southeast Asia where valuable silks, spices, and jewelry were produced.

One of the most determined adventurers was named Christopher Columbus. An Italian by birth, he was sponsored by King Ferdinand and Queen Isabella, joint rulers of Spain. Columbus hoped to reach the rich lands of Asia by traveling west. He had no idea when he first set sail in 1492 that he would encounter a whole "New World," which is what Europeans called the Americas.

When Ponce de León volunteered to sail on Columbus's second voyage in 1493, he was taking a bold step into the unknown. Sea voyages were dangerous, and there was no certainty that he would reach his destination.

LIFE ONBOARD SHIP

Compared with modern ocean-going vessels, the ships sailed by 15th- and 16th-century explorers were small, slow, and fragile. We do not know which of Columbus's ships Ponce de León traveled on, but it was probably one of the smaller or less seaworthy vessels, since, in 1493, Ponce de León was only an ordinary foot soldier.

All the ships were made from wooden planks held together by wooden pegs and iron nails. They had no motors but were powered by the wind trapped in heavy canvas sails that were raised and lowered by sailors.

European sailing ships had to wait for favorable winds to blow them westward to the Americas or eastward back to Europe. If the winds dropped and there was calm, they could not move far. If the winds blew too strongly — and Columbus's route from Spain to the Caribbean passed through a hurricane zone — they were likely to capsize and sink. With good luck and fair weather, it took a small ship between 20 and 30 days to reach the Americas from Spain.

Conditions on board the ships were dark, damp, cold, cramped, and smelly. Almost everyone fell ill, either from seasickness or drinking dirty water and eating rotting food. Typical meals were hard biscuits and stringy dried beef.

Christopher Columbus is often celebrated as the first European to reach the Americas, but Vikings landed in Canada almost 500 years before him.

Tallahassee

St. Augustine

FLORIDA

Miami

Havana

Tropic of Cancer

B I M I N I

BAHAMAS

ATLANTIC OCEAN

CUBA

HISPANIOLA

HAITI

DOMINICAN REPUBLIC

CARIBBEAN SEA

JAMAICA

LOCAL PEOPLE

Many different Native American peoples lived in Florida, Bimini, and the Caribbean, including the Taino, Carib, Caloosa, and Ciboney people. These Natives made long canoe journeys to fight and to trade. Ponce de León first met them when he arrived from Spain in 1483.

BIMINI

Bimini is a Native term for the Bahamas and other islands nearby. In 1513, Ponce de León sailed here with about 50 companions on board three small ships — the *Santa María de la Consolación*, the *Santiago*, and the *San Cristóbal*. He returned on a second and final voyage in 1521.

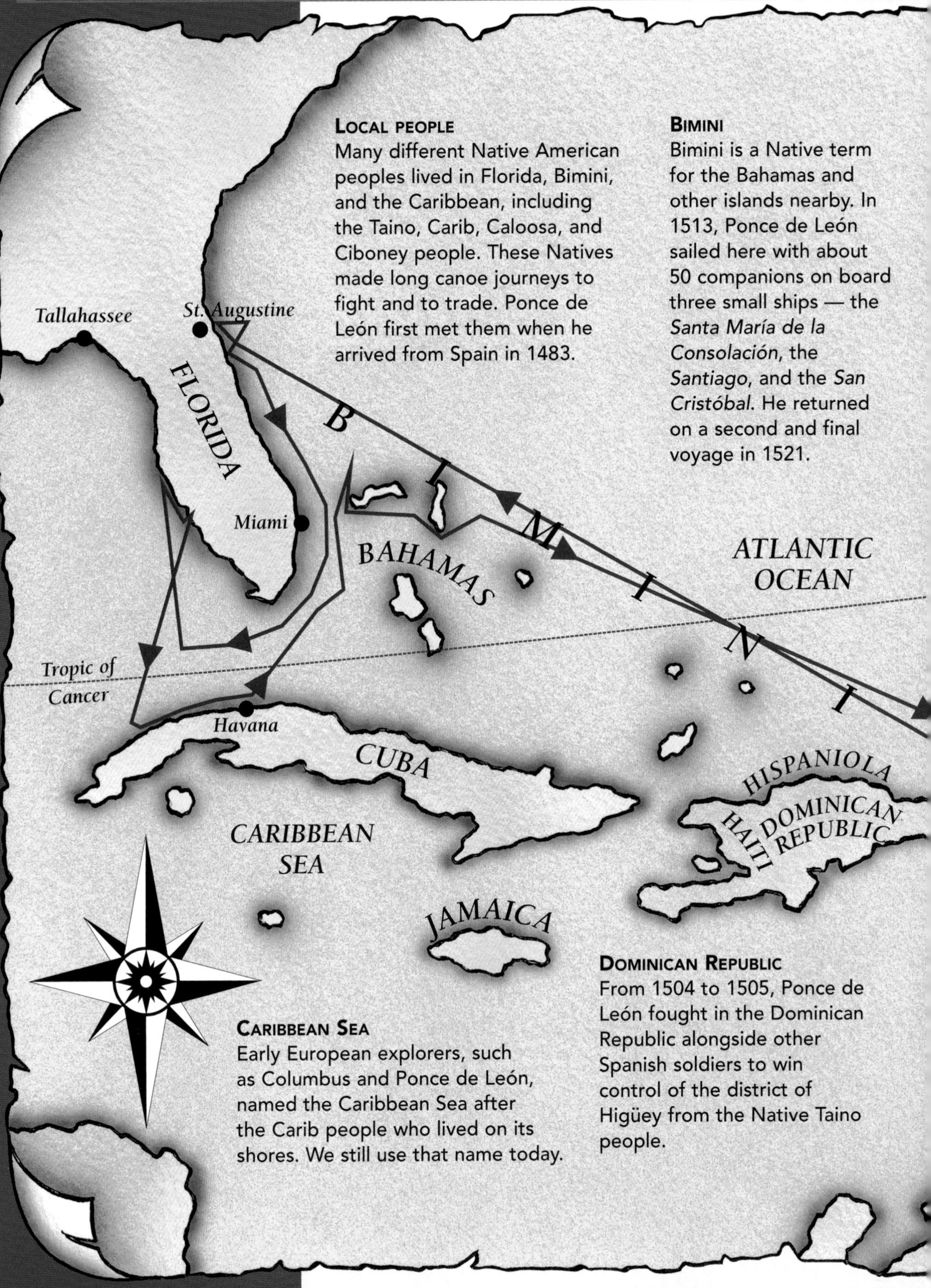

CARIBBEAN SEA

Early European explorers, such as Columbus and Ponce de León, named the Caribbean Sea after the Carib people who lived on its shores. We still use that name today.

DOMINICAN REPUBLIC

From 1504 to 1505, Ponce de León fought in the Dominican Republic alongside other Spanish soldiers to win control of the district of Higüey from the Native Taino people.

PONCE DE LEÓN'S
CAREER IN THE NEW WORLD

THREE NAMES
Throughout their history, many places on this map have had at least three names — Native, Spanish (used by explorers like Columbus and Ponce de León), and present day.

FIRST IN FLORIDA
Ponce de León was not the first European to visit Florida. Columbus saw it but did not land in 1492, and Spanish slave traders visited it in 1511.

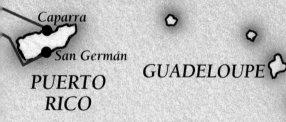

Caparra

San Germán

PUERTO RICO

GUADELOUPE

PUERTO RICO
From 1509 to 1511, Ponce de León was temporary governor of Puerto Rico and commander of the resident Spanish army. Here he cleared a new farm, built another house, supervised the digging of gold mines, and founded a city at Caparra. He set out from Puerto Rico on his historic voyage to Florida in 1513.

This map shows the places where Ponce de León lived and traveled during his career in the New World. He first set foot on the island of Puerto Rico (then known as Borinquén) in December 1493 when Columbus's second fleet stopped there. From Puerto Rico, the ships sailed to La Navidad in Haiti (then known as Bohio), where Columbus had left a few sailors the year before to build a village. Columbus, Ponce de León, and their companions found all those sailors killed, apparently at the hands of local people, and their houses destroyed. We are not certain of Ponce de León's movements during the next few years. He might have returned to Spain with Columbus in 1494. He was next heard from in Higüey, now in the Dominican Republic, possibly in 1502 but certainly in 1504. From that time on, he spent almost his entire life in the New World, fighting, farming, and exploring, until his death in 1521.

KEY
——— *Voyage of 1513*

RULERS OF THE WORLD

The stance taken by Ponce de León in this statue (*right*) suggests total allegiance to the monarchy of Castile by a proud and loyal subject.

European explorers relied on kings and queens to sponsor, or support, their explorations. In return, the rulers hoped to gain new lands, wealth, and power.

Christopher Columbus and Juan Ponce de León are often called the "discoverers" of Florida, the Bahamas, and the islands of the Caribbean. This is not really true. All these places were well-known to Native peoples who had lived there for centuries before European explorers arrived; but to Columbus, Ponce de León, and all the other soldiers and settlers who sailed with them, these lands on the far side of the Atlantic Ocean were new, unknown, mysterious, and exciting. Just as important, they were rich new territories that could be conquered to provide a profit for the Europeans and bring wealth and glory to King Ferdinand, Queen Isabella, and the kings and queens who would rule Spain after them.

This map (*left*) shows the island of Guadeloupe from where Ponce de León is said to have fled from a Carib attack. The event occurred in 1515, a time between his two voyages to Florida.

ROYAL PATRONAGE

King Ferdinand and Queen Isabella encouraged exploration by Spanish sailors. The king and queen wanted to conquer more lands than their great rival Portugal and build up a mighty Spanish empire in distant parts of the world. Therefore, they helped pay for many European explorers' expeditions, including Columbus's first voyage.

> ❝ *You may go and look for this place with ships, but it shall be at your own cost. For this, you [Ponce de León] can have three years.* ❞
>
> KING FERDINAND

The ships and supplies needed for long ocean voyages were expensive. Each ship cost about as much as a jet airplane does today. Money was also necessary for food and wages for the explorers and their crews, but explorers had to take with them almost everything else they would need as well, including weapons, armor, horses, carts, clothes, shoes, medicines, cooking pots, and farm tools.

Spanish kings and queens also granted licenses to explorers, giving them royal permission to explore and take control of "unknown" areas in the New World — but at their own expense.

KEEPING THE LAW

No explorer was allowed to set out on an expedition without a royal license, because Spanish kings and queens wanted to keep control of their explorers' actions overseas. They realized that far away from Spain it would be very easy for cruel, greedy, or selfish explorers to break the law and cheat or harass Native peoples in the New World. It would also be easy for new explorers to attack peaceful European sailors they met on their voyages. Explorers were usually well equipped with swords and guns, and they were not slow to use them.

Also, Spanish kings and queens wanted details about all the lands that Spanish explorers visited so that any "new" territory could be formally claimed for Spain. In this way, the kings and queens could demand their share of riches from the conquered lands.

In return for royal sponsorship or royal license, explorers were expected to send back regular cargoes of gold, jewels, exotic produce,

CHIEF SPANISH EXPLORATIONS IN THE NEW WORLD

1492–1493
Columbus to the Bahamas and Cuba.

1493–1494
Columbus to Haiti and Cuba.

1498
Columbus to Trinidad and Venezuela.

1501–1502
Bastidas and La Cosa to Venezuela and Panama.

1502–1504
Columbus to Honduras, Nicaragua, and Panama.

1508
Pinzón and Solis to southeast coast of Mexico.

1513
Ponce de León to the Bahamas and Florida.

1517
Hernandez de Cordoba to Cuba and southeast Mexico.

1518
Crijavala to Mexico.

1519
Pineda to Mexico and Florida.

1519
Cortés to Mexico.

1521
Ponce de León to Florida.

and captive Native American people who would be sold in European slave markets.

A NEW EMPIRE

According to Spanish law, all land conquered by Spanish soldiers belonged to the Spanish crown. As explorers from Spain began to take control of islands and groups of islands in the Caribbean, Spanish kings, Spanish queens, and the whole Spanish nation became extremely rich.

Teams of colonial administrators ruled new territory on behalf of their monarchs, because kings and queens far away in Spain could not control all the newly conquered lands in their empire. They appointed men they could trust to administer the law and ordered them to send regular reports back to Spain. Each team of colonial administrators was headed by a *viceroy*, or "deputy king" — a position of great prestige and power.

As a sign of their approval for his ambitious plans, King Ferdinand and Queen Isabella appointed Christopher Columbus viceroy of all the lands he might one day conquer before he set sail on his first transatlantic voyage. When Christopher Columbus died in 1506, his son Diego claimed the right to become viceroy after him. Many people opposed Diego, but he won this right in 1511 and held the post until his death in 1526.

As part of the same system of overseas empire government, King Ferdinand and Queen Isabella appointed Ponce de León *adelantado*, or "frontier governor" of the Higüey district (in present-day Dominican Republic) in 1504. His duties included holding law courts, commanding Spanish soldiers, and defending lands conquered for Spain from Native attack.

Like other government officials in the so-called New World, Ponce de León was meant to take orders from viceroys. Christopher and

If not for the jealousy of Diego Columbus, seen here as a boy at a monastery with his father (*above*), Ponce de León might never have left Puerto Rico to reach Florida.

An early map of Puerto Rico (*left*).

Diego Columbus were often away on voyages or back home in Europe, however, so in practice, Ponce de León was usually able to make his own decisions and to govern in the way he thought best.

DIVIDING THE NEW WORLD

Spanish rulers had another reason for their interest in the actions of explorers overseas. They did not want to be pushed unprepared into a quarrel with other nations. A fight over land or treasure between Spanish and Portuguese sailors in the Caribbean might easily have provoked a European war. To prevent this from happening, the rulers of Spain and Portugal signed the Treaty of Tordesillas in 1489. In it, they agreed to divide all New World territory between them. Portugal was to rule land east of an imaginary line that ran from the tip of Newfoundland in North America to the Amazon River estuary in South America. Spain was to rule land to the west.

This division of the New World between Spain and Portugal explains why most people in South and Central America speak Spanish today — because these lands were once conquered and ruled by Spain — but Brazilians, whose land was conquered by Portugal, speak Portuguese.

On arrival in Florida, Ponce de León discovered that the Tainos excelled at fishing, as seen in this image (*above*). No doubt they caught many species that were new to Ponce de León.

" **I [the King] grant you [Ponce de León] the title of Governor of this place and any other places you may discover.** "
KING FERDINAND

FANTASY AND CURIOSITY

The kings and queens who sponsored New World explorers hoped that they would investigate old myths and legends and discover new scientific information.

Even a conqueror as bold in battle as Alexander the Great, depicted here (*below*) in a mosaic from Pompeii dating from the second century B.C., is said to have believed in the existence of miraculous waters that would make him immortal. They were never found for him, however, and he was to die young, living from 356 to 323 B.C.

In Ponce de León's time, people looked at the world in a very different way than we do today. Almost everyone then believed in some form of magic, witchcraft, ghosts, curses, and charms. Europeans were fascinated by traditional myths and legends. They may not have believed every detail, but they thought that some of the tales might, in part, be true.

Europeans were also fascinated by the stories brought back from distant lands by travelers. Reports of Columbus's voyages quickly became bestsellers, and everyone was eager to hear more exciting tales about the New World.

THE FOUNTAIN OF YOUTH

King Ferdinand, Ponce de León's sponsor, was particularly interested in stories from the Caribbean. These stories described a mysterious "Fountain of Youth." Explorers claimed that this fountain could be found in or around Bimini. They based their claims on traditional tales told by the Taino people of Cuba. These tales told about a spring with the magical power to make old people young again. Ponce de León must have heard these tales, but we do not know whether or not he believed they were true.

> **He knew from the natives of a fountain with waters that could turn men into boys.**

Myths featuring magic waters existed in many different civilizations, probably because the cleansing and refreshing qualities of water are appreciated by all human beings. King Ferdinand would have known at least one European magic waters story, which told how the ancient Greek hero Alexander the Great bathed with his soldiers in the Euphrates River (in what is now Iraq). The soldiers were all weak and exhausted

after a battle, but the river restored them to health and strength. This story was almost 2,000 years old by Ponce de León's time, but it was still popular.

HOPES FOR A SON

The reports of a Fountain of Youth in Bimini may have held an extra meaning for King Ferdinand of Spain. He was growing old and his health was poor. Queen Isabella had died in 1504, leaving no son to rule after King Ferdinand, so in 1512, at age sixty, Ferdinand married a new young wife. He hoped that water from the Fountain of Youth, if it could be found, would make him feel young and strong again and help him father a child.

From the Ganges River in India to the Canary Islands off Africa, enchanted waters (*above*) that would grant eternal youth were said to exist.

The desire to find miraculous places is common to the legends of many cultures. In a Greek myth, for example, Heracles sets out to find the golden apples created for the goddess Hera and guarded by the three Hesperides in their garden, as depicted in this painting by Edward Burne-Jones (*left*).

QUESTIONING TRADITIONAL BELIEFS

NEW QUESTIONS, NEW IDEAS

By 1500, educated people in many European countries were beginning to challenge some traditional, superstitious beliefs and to ask searching questions about the world around them. They were a small minority of the total population, but their ideas were increasingly powerful. They encouraged astronomers and geographers to make new and more accurate observations of Earth and the sky and prompted explorers, including Ponce de León, to investigate distant lands.

Scholars and scientists also helped explorers develop new navigational and mapmaking techniques. In turn, these made it easier for sailors to plan long voyages and to keep detailed records of all they had seen on their travels.

This detail from a 16th-century map (*above*) shows some of the places close to Florida where the Fountain of Youth was probably sought.

MIXED MOTIVES

We do not know what Ponce de León thought about traditional myths and magic, but he must have come into contact with many new scientific ideas when he traveled with Christopher Columbus and when he met other explorers in the New World.

His own experiences of the climate, wildlife, landscape, and Native civilizations in the Caribbean — all very different from what he had known in Spain — may also have encouraged him to re-examine some of his earlier views and beliefs. Probably, like many other 16th-century people, Ponce de León was able to look at the world in two different ways — traditional and questioning.

The European rulers who sponsored explorers' voyages also shared this mixed view of the world. They wanted scientific information, but they also wanted to hear entertaining travelers' tales.

EL DORADO

Like other European rulers, King Ferdinand was intrigued by travelers' tales about *El Dorado*, a place somewhere in the New World immensely rich in gold and ruled over by a magical golden king.

All European kings and queens, and most European explorers, were greedy to find gold. It was the most precious metal known, and they hoarded it as a national treasure. The ruler who could get the most gold from the New World would be the richest and most powerful. The explorer who found El Dorado would win fame and fortune forever.

EXPLORATIONS AND EXPLANATIONS

No explorer ever found El Dorado or the mysterious Fountain of Youth. Almost certainly, they did not exist — at least, not in the way they were described in colorful travelers' tales. Historians do think that stories about El Dorado and the Fountain of Youth might have been based on facts that were greatly exaggerated and distorted by European misunderstanding of Native American civilizations.

The myth of El Dorado may have come from customs of Native peoples who lived in the lands now known as Colombia and Venezuela.

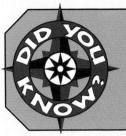

Ponce de León had hoped to discover gold, as well as the Fountain of Youth, in Florida. King Ferdinand died before Ponce de Léon's second voyage, and so he never knew if Ponce de León ever succeeded in locating the Fountain of Youth or the gold.

As expert gold workers, they made lifelike golden figures as offerings to their gods. Kings taking part in religious ceremonies may also have been sprinkled with real powdered gold.

Possible explanations for the story of the Fountain of Youth also exist. In Florida, there are many natural springs that bubble up from the ground at a temperature of about 68° Fahrenheit (38° Celsius) and that feel pleasantly cool in Florida's warm climate. Also, fresh water was scarce or unobtainable on many nearby islands, but the spring water was pure and safe to drink. Therefore, Native American people may have considered Florida a place where one could live well.

Natural water holes called *cenotes* also had a spiritual significance in many parts of the New World. They were honored and feared as doorways into a magical supernatural world.

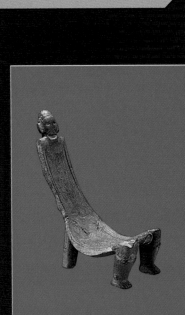

Two Taino artifacts, a carved wooden chair (*above*) and an amulet made from shell and shaped like a skull (*below*).

GOVERNOR, FARMER, FATHER

After several years away, Ponce De León returned to the New World. He settled there and raised a family on a royal farm in the Dominican Republic.

Columbus, shown sighting land in this print (*above*), undoubtedly provided the inspiration for Ponce de León to go to sea.

Spanish kings and queens intended to make the best economic use of all their New World lands. To achieve this, they gave large farms in conquered countries to explorers, soldiers, settlers, and other people whom they wished to help or reward. In 1504, King Ferdinand and Queen Isabella gave Ponce de León a farm in Higüey to thank him for fighting against the local Taino people.

These royal farms were called *encomiendas*. They had a minimum size of 225 acres (91 hectares) but were often much larger. We are not sure exactly how much land Ponce de León was given, but we do know that it was good for farming, with fertile land and an excellent water supply.

Spanish kings and queens also gave Ponce de León and other landowners the right to recruit a workforce of Native American people to work on their land.

> ❝ *To bestow my favor on you, I grant you the authority to discover and settle the islands of Bimini.* ❞
> KING FERDINAND

A GOOD EMPLOYER?

No reliable evidence survives to tell us how Ponce de León behaved toward the workers on his farm, but most

This crest (*left*) dates from 1497 and is that of King Ferdinand and Queen Isabella of Castile, who gave royal backing to Ponce de León.

Some Europeans saw Native Americans as "savages." Today, we find these attitudes shocking and unacceptable, but they were widely accepted by Europeans in Ponce de León's time.

historians suggest that he treated them fairly well in comparison with the standards of his time. As a local governor, Ponce de León would have been aware of the Spanish laws that existed to protect workers on the farms of settlers. He knew that if he broke these laws, a rival might send reports back to Spain. The king and queen might then dismiss him from his post and possibly even take his farm away.

MISCONCEPTIONS

Sixteenth-century Spanish law-makers assumed that Native American people were like children who needed European guidance, guardianship, and control. Under Spanish rule, Natives were not free to do what they wanted and had no civil rights, but otherwise they were supposed to be treated kindly.

A SUCCESSFUL FARMER

We know much more about the way in which Ponce de León ran his farm. He chose a site on the banks of a river leading to a sheltered bay where Spanish ships heading back for Europe stopped to buy last-minute supplies. Here, he was able to sell food and water to sailors at a high price.

While most European settlers remained ignorant of Native culture, beliefs, and traditions, Ponce de León seems to have been a rare exception. He must have carefully studied Taino farming techniques and aspects of their lifestyle, because he decided to grow local food crops on his farm, rather than plant wheat, barley, and other seeds imported from Europe. He judged correctly that local plants were much more likely to thrive in the tropical

WORKERS OR SLAVES?

Spanish landowners who farmed in the New World were allowed to take their workers from local villages. If the Natives agreed to leave their homes and families peacefully, Spanish law stated that they should receive food, housing, and wages in return for their work. All too often, though, Native workers were very badly treated.

By 1504, when Ponce de León was given his royal farm, there were already examples of slavery in the New World. According to Spanish law, Native Americans who fought against European settlers could be captured and sold as slaves. Spanish kings and queens encouraged European traders to bring slaves (*below*) from West Africa across the Atlantic Ocean to work on farms throughout South America and the Caribbean.

After Ferdinand died in 1516, Ponce de León had to ask for help from the king's grandson Carlos (*right*), who became King of Spain and then, in 1519, Holy Roman Emperor.

Ponce de León received no financial support from the new monarch Carlos, who is pictured on this silver coin (*left*).

Vicente Pinzón (*below*) failed to colonize Puerto Rico, helping Ponce de León become governor in his place.

conditions of Higüey and that the Native American workers on his farm would have the skills and experience to tend them.

The chief crop grown on Ponce de León's farm was cassava, a starchy root that could be dried and made into bread. This stayed edible for weeks, even onboard ship. He also grew sweet potatoes (a favorite food native to the Americas), squash, and other local vegetables, and he raised European animals, including horses, pigs, and cattle, to provide meat for Spanish settlers and sailors.

A GOOD MARRIAGE

By the end of 1504, life seemed to be going very well for Ponce de León. He had proved his skill and courage as a soldier by fighting to protect Spanish conquests in Higüey. He had been appointed to a senior position in the overseas service of the Spanish king and queen. He had been given a farm, which he hoped would make him rich, and he had plans to build a house there. Now he was turning 30 years old — the traditional age of maturity for a 16th-century European man. It was time for Ponce de León to find a wife and raise a family. Sons and daughters would preserve his memory and pass on his name to future generations.

Spanish society was known throughout Europe for its rigid class system. Spanish noble families, such as Ponce de León's, were aware of their high rank and social status. They liked to keep separate from ordinary people even if, like Ponce de León's parents, they were powerless and poor.

Spanish explorers and settlers carried this strict class system with them to the Caribbean and South America. They also made race a factor in the class system. They believed that white people born to Spanish parents in Spain were better than anyone born in the New World.

Ponce de León was not likely to challenge this class system, because, as a

> *I shall report to Your Majesty on everything I find, and shall ask for financial help. I hope it will be granted to me because I can't imagine undertaking such an expedition without reward. I kiss your royal feet and hands.*

Without favors originally granted by Queen Isabella, pictured here with King Ferdinand (*below*), neither Columbus nor Ponce de León would have reached the New World.

nobleman, he benefited from it. Therefore, from his point of view, there were few suitable women to marry. Hardly any European women had traveled to the New World at that time. Ponce de León probably did not consider a Native American for a bride, although many Native American women were companions to Spanish explorers.

Ponce de León did marry. He chose Leónor, daughter of a Spanish innkeeper in the town of Santo Domingo (now in the Dominican Republic). Hoping to make his fortune, Leónor's father had moved his family there. Compared to Ponce de León's noble ancestors, Leónor's family was humble, but at least she had been born in Spain.

We do not know whether Ponce de León and Leónor loved one another. At that time, few people thought that romantic love was essential in marriage. They had four children — Juana, Isabel, Maria, and Luis — and their descendants lived in the New World for the next 400 years.

A NEW TOWN
To house his growing family, Ponce de León built an impressive new stone house in Higüey. He called it Salvaleón, after his family's estate in Spain, and got permission from the rulers of Spain to build a new town (also called Salvaleón) close by. This was a shrewd business venture, because towns gave their founders the chance to make money through trade and by renting out houses.

TO PUERTO RICO AND FLORIDA

Ponce de León left his family and farm to set out on further voyages of exploration, looking for islands but finding mainland North America, instead.

Not only did Ponce de León and his crew have to face forceful currents, they also sometimes met with pirates (*above*) who would try to attack a larger ship to take possession of their supplies and trading goods.

Balboa (*right*) founded a settlement on Panama and was the first European to see the Pacific Ocean. He was a friend of Ponce de León, yet it seems against all odds that they should both have become governors on the same day.

The island of Borinquén (called San Juan Bautista by Spanish explorers and Puerto Rico today) lay about 70 miles (113 kilometers) east of Ponce de León's farm at Salvaleón in Higüey. Christopher Columbus had stopped at Borinquén briefly in 1493, and Native Taino people regularly traveled between its western coast and Higüey. The Natives brought with them tales about streams rich in nuggets of gold and local people who had gold jewelry to barter cheaply.

As a shrewd businessman, Ponce de León was interested in these stories, so in 1508, he planned a voyage to Puerto Rico, intending to conquer it for Spain and to find gold for himself and his family. He may have made an earlier voyage to the island in 1506 to have a first look.

THE RIGHT TO RULE
By 1508, Ponce de León had another reason for leaving Higüey. His sponsor, King Ferdinand, was involved in a legal quarrel with Diego Columbus, son of the famous explorer Christopher Columbus. Diego had claimed the right by inheritance to be viceroy of all the lands his father had explored. King Ferdinand was not happy with this arrangement, because he would have liked to have

appointed men whom he knew and trusted, such as Ponce de León, instead.

Diego Columbus's home base in the New World was in the Dominican Republic. He had not, so far, interfered with Ponce de León's local governorship in Higüey, but there was a constant threat that he might do so. Ponce de León seems, therefore, to have decided to move away and settle on another island, where he would be free to govern the local people and run his farm in his own way.

Secretly, King Ferdinand agreed with Ponce de León's plans. In 1509, the king appointed Ponce de León temporary governor of Puerto Rico and, in 1510, commander of the army and navy there as well as chief justice.

NEW FARMS, NEW TOWNS

In Puerto Rico, Ponce de León did not find much gold, even though he organized prospecting expeditions to the interior of the island and opened up several mines. He did, however, build new towns, including a capital city for the island, which he named Caparra. It was sited about 10 miles (16 km) away from San Juan, the present capital of Puerto Rico.

Ponce de León also introduced the *encomienda* system of farming, and the *repartimiento* system of forcing local Native people to work on settlers' farms.

Some historians have suggested that most local Taino people were willing to accept Spanish rule, because Spanish soldiers protected the Tainos from their old enemies, the Caribs. Spanish settlers did cause great suffering among the Tainos, however, by introducing European diseases such as measles and smallpox to local people who had no resistance to them. As a result, many Taino families died.

Skirmishes with Indian encampments, like this one in a lithograph (*above*), continued long after Ponce de León had died.

Taino villages were quite large and often grouped around large ceremonial plazas (*below*).

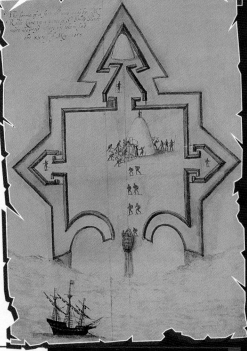

> ❝ *They named this place [now Florida Keys] The Martyrs because many people were known to have lost their lives there.* ❞
> HERRERA Y TORDESILLAS

The survivors were not well treated by Spanish settlers, and in 1511, the remaining Tainos rebelled. Ponce de León and all the other Spaniards had to fight for their lives. They survived but with difficulty.

At the end of 1511, Diego Columbus won his lawsuit against King Ferdinand. Right away, he dismissed Ponce de León as governor of Puerto Rico. It was time for Ponce de León to go.

TO BIMINI

King Ferdinand still admired Ponce de León and wished to help him. He suggested that Ponce de León explore islands where Diego Columbus had no right to be viceroy and establish new Spanish colonies there. If Ponce de León claimed these lands for Spain, King Ferdinand promised to appoint him governor. By 1511, several other Spanish explorers were active in the New World, but none of them had chosen to explore, in a systematic way, the seas north of the Bahamas. In 1512, Ponce de León received a license from King Ferdinand in Spain, giving him permission to explore the land of Bimini.

LAND OF FLOWERS

It took several months to recruit a crew and prepare ships for the voyage. Ponce de León finally set sail early in March 1513. Like all other Spaniards at that time, he believed that Bimini was one of a chain of islands that included the Bahamas. He sailed past them and in April 1513, reached what he thought was the most northerly island in the chain. Landing near present-day Daytona Beach, he named the land *Florida*, meaning the "Flowery Place," because of its beautiful springtime blooms. He also gave Spanish names to many of the smaller islands he passed by.

Parts of the Florida Everglades must have looked much the same at the time of Ponce de León as they do today (*above*). He and the Castilian settlers would have come across swampy ground, yet no surviving records describe their attempts to travel through this sort of terrain.

66 *Because of the storms they were held back, and had to wait for 27 days before proceeding.* 99

At first, Ponce de León did not realize that Florida was part of the mainland — he still thought it was an island. He did learn from a Native American woman that it was not part of Bimini. She told him that it was a separate country, which Native people called Cautió.

NEW ARRIVALS

In addition to providing Ponce de León with the opportunity to give Florida the name it is still known by today, his voyage was significant in another way. Although he was not the first European to set foot on mainland America, two of his crew may have been the first Africans to step onto American mainland soil.

Ponce de León spent the next few weeks exploring both sides of the Florida peninsula. His ships were approached several times by Native people. Mostly they were hostile — probably because they had been attacked by slave traders from Europe just two years earlier. Ponce de León also took some Native men and women prisoners. He hoped they would provide him with local information and act as interpreters. Twice, his sailors and Native people fought fierce battles. The Spaniards were armed with powerful guns and crossbows, however, which eventually drove the Native warriors away.

COMING HOME

On his journey home, Ponce de León explored the north coast of Cuba before returning to Puerto Rico in October 1515. Ponce de León returned home to find a crisis awaiting. While he had been away, Native Caribs had attacked Puerto Rico, burned Caparra, and destroyed his home and his farm. His family was safe, but his enemy, Diego Columbus, wanted to move Ponce de León's home and the homes of other Spanish settlers to a less desirable part of the island, so that Columbus could take over their lands and turn their Taino farm workers into slaves.

Ponce de León needed to safeguard his government posts and his family's future, so he traveled to Spain to meet with King Ferdinand. The king continued to support Ponce de León and encouraged him to make a second trip to Florida as soon as possible. Before Ponce de León could organize a new expedition, however, Ferdinand died.

A SECOND VOYAGE

After his first voyage to Florida, Ponce de León visited King Ferdinand, who welcomed him warmly and was eager to hear news about Florida. King Ferdinand made Ponce de León a knight and gave him a large sum of money as a sign of his approval. The king also suggested that Ponce de León plan a second voyage to Florida as soon as possible. As a final honor, King Ferdinand named Ponce de León governor of Florida and gave him the sole right to explore it and colonize it for Spain.

LOCAL INHABITANTS

When European explorers first arrived in the New World, they encountered thriving local communities of Native American people.

A European artist's conception of a Timuca Indian in Florida (*above*) about the time of Ponce de León.

In Florida, Ponce de León met men and women belonging to the Caloosa or Timuca people, who were related to other Native American groups that had lived in the southeastern region of North America for thousands of years. On each of his voyages, Ponce de León saw very little of Florida, apart from the coast. If he had ventured inland, he would have found civilizations based on hunting, fishing, and farming. Maize, or corn, was the most important crop and was planted by the women, who prepared the ground for the seeds using hoes with heads made of sharp fish bones.

The Native peoples of the southeast region were also skilled craftworkers, who made beautiful pottery and ornaments of carved and

When colonizing Puerto Rico and Florida, Castilians would have seen Indian villages similar to the one shown in this illustration (*left*). Such a group of dwellings was often surrounded by protective wooden fencing.

> **They are so ingenious and free with all they have that . . . if it be asked of them . . . they invite you to share it and show as much love as if their hearts went with it.**
>
> CHRISTOPHER COLUMBUS, COMMENTING ON THE GENEROUS WELCOME GIVEN BY THE TAINOS TO THE FIRST EUROPEANS TO VISIT THEIR ISLANDS.

THE TAINO PEOPLE

Christopher Columbus met the Taino people before Ponce de León. He described them as attractive, well fed, and healthy looking. He reported that Taino men and women were all mostly under 5 feet 6 inches (1.5 meters 15.2 centimeters) tall, of muscular build, with smooth, olive-brown or copper-colored skin and thick black hair. Their hair was cut short around the face but left to grow long at the back.

The weather is warm all year in the Caribbean region, so Taino people did not feel the need to wear many clothes. Children and young people went naked, men wore simple loinclothes, and women wore short skirts made of cotton cloth. Village elders, clan chiefs, and religious leaders wore decorated cloaks or tunics when taking part in important festivals or religious ceremonies.

polished shells. They wore few clothes, apart from feather cloaks, but decorated their skins all over with elaborate tattoos. They set up long-distance trading networks and built large villages and towns. The huge earth mounds, which they constructed as sites for their holy temples, still survive today.

MANY PEOPLES

In the Caribbean, Ponce de León met the Taino people, who lived throughout the region, the Ciboney and Guanahatabey peoples, who lived in western Cuba, and the Macorix and Ciguayo peoples, who lived in Haiti and the Dominican Republic. He also encountered, and perhaps fought against, the Caribs who lived in the cluster of islands known today as the Lesser Antilles, which includes the Virgin Islands and the Windward and Leeward Islands.

A RICH ENVIRONMENT

So many different groups of Native American people lived in the Caribbean region, because it was a very rich environment that provided everything they needed to survive. Over the centuries, many families of farmers and fishermen had migrated to make new homes there. Historians think that most Caribbean settlers came from the northernmost regions of South America. They were attracted by the islands' warm, moist climate, the abundant wildlife (on land and in the surrounding seas), and the luxuriant vegetation that flourished in their fertile soils.

VILLAGE HOMES

The Taino people lived in large villages sited in sheltered river valleys and along the coast. Some housed over a thousand people. Village homes were made of palm-tree trunks lashed together with plant-

This plan of an Indian settlement (*left*) was drawn by John White at the end of the 16th century.

fiber rope and thatched with dried grass. They were usually rectangular or, occasionally, circular. All village buildings were neatly arranged around a large open square. This space was used for community religious ceremonies, which included singing and dancing, mock battles, and ballgames.

GREAT LEADERS

Each village or group of villages was led by a chief, and each district of an island was governed by a senior chief, known in the Taino language as a "caique." At the time Ponce de León arrived, five caiques ruled in Haiti and the Dominican Republic and twenty in Puerto Rico. All chiefs and caiques had religious, as well as practical, responsibilities. Together with priests they sacrificed some of the first crops each season to the gods and goddesses who helped them grow, sought help and guidance from ancestor spirits, and arranged the community festivals.

FIELDS AND FARMS

Each Taino village was surrounded by fields, where farmers grew crops of maize, cassava, and beans. On some islands, growing crops were kept supplied with water by cleverly designed irrigation ditches.

Although men usually cleared fields from the dense rain forest — slashing the dense undergrowth and uprooting tree stumps — women did much of the farm work, especially at harvest time. Grains, herbs, and cassava tubers were all carefully dried, then stored away in dark, dry sheds for future use. Women also tended fruit trees and gathered nuts and the roots of wild plants. Taino people were skilled at using many different plants to make medicines and also dyes to color feathers that were used for decoration and cotton cloth.

FISH AND FOWLS

For meat, the Taino people relied on wild birds, fish, and other sea creatures. Villagers kept flocks of tame

This Taino bone pipe may have been used in spiritual ceremonies.

DID YOU KNOW?

At the time when Ponce de León first visited the Caribbean, the Taino people formed the largest and most powerful group of Native Americans living there. In the Tainos' own language, their name meant "good."

ducks (which they ate roasted) and sent boys and young men to hunt wildfowl in the forests. They also caught and ate giant turtles, manatees, and shellfish that lived in the shallow waters around the islands' coasts.

USEFUL AND BEAUTIFUL

Taino craftworkers wove cotton and other plant fibers into ropes, hammocks (which the Tainos used instead of beds for sleeping), mats, baskets, and many other useful items. Spanish sailors arriving in the New World admired the well-made Taino fishing nets they found there, carefully knotted and woven from rope.

Taino boatbuilders dug out the trunks of huge rainforest trees to make canoes big enough to carry 100 people and fitted them with woven cotton sails. Canoes like this were used to carry people on long voyages between the islands. For fishing trips upriver and around the coast, Tainos used smaller, lighter canoes. Taino carpenters carved chairs and made wooden spears and digging tools. Potters shaped beautiful bowls out of clay and decorated them with magic patterns. Jewelers made beads and pendants from shells and bones. They also made earrings, nose plugs, and necklaces out of glittering gold.

MYTHS AND LEGENDS

The Taino people had many marvelous myths and legends. One told that they were descended from a hero called Deminian Caracaracol who married a female turtle. They honored these ancestors and others in religious ceremonies.

Another legend described how, at night, the dark, watery underworld rose above ground to become the night sky. The stars were all the sea creatures, such as crabs and lobsters, who lived there — the Milky Way was a giant alligator.

WORDS WE LEARNED FROM CARIBBEAN PEOPLES

European explorers in the New World saw many plants, animals, manufactured objects, and natural phenomena that they had never seen before. They did not know what they were, how they were made, or what caused them. They did not even have words to describe them! They asked local people what these interesting new things were called and learned their Native American names.

Over the centuries, many of these Caribbean words have become part of our regular English language. We still use them today. Barbecue, canoe, hammock, hurricane, maize, and maracas are some of the best-known words we have learned from the Taino, Carib, and other Native American people who spoke with European explorers like Ponce de León almost 500 years ago.

NATURAL WONDERS

Ponce de León made one very important scientific observation that is still of use today for sailors and for experts studying how our climate changes.

Thermal images are now widely used by scientists to show variations in temperature within the human body and in geographical regions. This picture (*above*) was taken from space and clearly shows where, along the east coast of the Florida peninsula, the warm waters of the Gulf Stream (red tones) meet colder waters (blue). It is the second-largest ocean current in the world and is so strong that sea captains sailing west from England were once advised, "Don't fight the Gulf Stream!"

European rulers were always pleased when the explorers whom they sponsored conquered new land and helped build vast empires. Looking back today, we can also see that these voyages made by 16th-century explorers were just as important in other ways. One of the most long-lasting results of their travels was a greatly improved understanding of geography and the natural world.

In Ponce de León's time, Europeans did not know that mainland North America existed, and they were only just beginning to explore the coast of South America. They had never seen potatoes, tomatoes, or tobacco, all of which were crops native to America that did not grow elsewhere.

Compared with today, Europeans also knew very little about winds, waves, ocean currents, and navigation. Sailors estimated their position at sea by using cross-staffs or astrolabes. Both relied on observations of the height of stars above the horizon to calculate distances traveled. Cross-staffs and astrolabes were difficult to use on the rolling deck of a ship at sea. As a result, navigation was imprecise. The usual directions given to sailors voyaging from Spain to the New World

At the time when Ponce de León sailed, the most accurate aid to navigation was a knowledge of astronomy. The instrument used to measure the position of the stars for this purpose was called an astrolabe (*right*).

> ## "We know the stream well because of our pursuit of whales."
> ### TIMOTHY FOLGER,
> #### 18TH-CENTURY AMERICAN SEA CAPTAIN

were to sail south until butter melts (or in other words, until the weather grew warm) and then head west.

FINDING OUT MORE

All European explorers wanted to learn more about the climatic and oceanic conditions that they might expect to encounter on their voyages. Columbus had noticed on each of his four voyages westward that steady trade winds blowing from the northeast could help push sailing ships across the Atlantic toward the Caribbean.

Explorers also knew that their lives might depend on choosing the right time to set sail. They needed to avoid winter storms in the Atlantic Ocean and summer hurricanes in the Caribbean. They all remembered how a Spanish fleet on its way to the New World had been stricken by a savage storm off the Canary Islands in February 1502, resulting in a tragic loss of life.

A RIVER IN THE SEA

Ponce de León had been one of the few lucky passengers to survive the 1502 shipwreck.

It seems reasonable to suggest that this might have left him with a personal interest in observing all that went on in the ocean, but we cannot be sure. We do know, however, that on his first voyage to Florida in 1513, Ponce de León observed one of the most important natural features in the whole Atlantic Ocean. This was a current, like a river in the sea, that flowed from the tip of Florida northeast to Europe.

THE GULF STREAM

Today, the current observed by Ponce de León is known as the Gulf Stream. Scientists think that it is part of a complex system of water circulation in the North and South Atlantic Oceans.

This circulation of water in the oceans is caused by strong winds blowing over land and sea and by differences in the

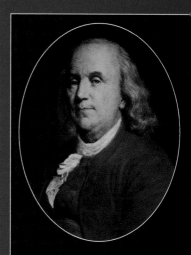

The 18th-century U.S. statesman and scientist Benjamin Franklin (*above*) took an interest in the Gulf Stream. A submersible, which explored the Gulf Stream waters in 1969, was named *Ben Franklin* in his honor.

The Isles of Scilly, off the coast of Cornwall, England, have surprisingly lush vegetation for this part of the world (*right*). It can all be attributed to the effects of the Gulf Stream.

Many people take a vacation in Florida (*left*), because chances are the weather will be fine; but nearby, out at sea, Ponce de León first met and fought with the Gulf Stream's strong current.

This map of the Caribbean and Venezuela (*below*), on the northern coast of South America, was made in about 1570. It also shows part of the east coast of North America along which the Gulf Stream flows.

Columbus sailed to the New World from Europe (*right*), taking advantage of the trade winds. A more favorable return route was used.

temperature of seawater as it flows closer to or farther away from the equator.

MASSIVE POWER

The Gulf Stream is a massive and powerful phenomenon. At the point off Florida where Ponce de León first saw it, the "river in the sea" measures about 40 miles (65 km) across and is 1,970 feet (600 m) deep. It moves four billion tons of water at the rate of 5 miles (8 km) per hour. Its surface temperature can reach 84° Fahrenheit (29° Celsius), and it often appears bright blue.

HINDRANCE OR HELP?

The Gulf Stream was more than just one more New World natural wonder. As soon as Ponce de León had reported

its existence, sailors and explorers realized that it would have a tremendous impact on shipping.

The Gulf Stream made east-west sea travel close to Florida extremely difficult. As one 16th-century writer commented, "So much water flowed there, and it was more forceful than the wind. Ships could not proceed, even if the sails were unfurled."

If ships wanted to sail northeast in the same direction as the Gulf Stream, however, they found that its strong current carried them along with ease and speed. In 1518, just five years after Ponce de León's first reports of the Gulf Stream, an experimental voyage proved that it could help ships sail much more quickly across the Atlantic Ocean to their destinations in Europe. This voyage was made by Spanish sailor Antón de Alaminos, one of Ponce de León's friends, who may have taken part in the historic voyage to Florida in 1513.

The Gulf Stream also saved many ships from disaster. Before they knew of its existence, sailors heading east to Europe often found themselves stuck in parts of the ocean where no winds blow for weeks at a time. They may also have struggled helplessly in the Bermuda

The Gulf Stream waters were difficult to navigate in the 16th century. A former member of Ponce de León's crew, Anton de Alaminos, rode the current successfully in 1518 and managed to bring back treasures from Mexico to the King of Spain.

Triangle — an area of sea close to the Bahamas that has since become famous as a place where many ships have mysteriously disappeared.

MONSTERS AND MERMAIDS

As well as reporting the existence of the Gulf Stream, Spanish explorers in the New World brought back to Europe many reports of strange creatures. They saw huge alligators lurking in creeks and swamps along the Florida coast. To sailors, these looked like dragons from myths and legends. They also reported *mandrakes*, or "trees with roots shaped like men," that were said to scream when they were pulled from the marshy ground. These were probably mangroves, a species of tree with roots specially adapted to grow in saltwater marshes.

Sailing ships might also be followed by sharks or flying fish that leaped and swooped above the surface of the waves, using their fins like wings. In the Sargasso Sea, they saw the ocean covered with vast mats of seaweed, as if it were overgrown with grass.

Closer to land, Ponce de León saw giant turtles. He named one group of islands near Florida Las Tortugas, after the turtles he saw there. He also saw manatees — huge, gentle, slow-moving mammals, shaped like seals. They made a moaning, sighing sound that traveled a good distance at sea. From afar, these manatees could be mistaken for humans. Historians think that manatees might have been the origin of tales about sirens and mermaids.

> **The next day, they followed the coast and met a current against which they could not sail although there was a favorable wind. . . . One ship was dragged to sea and vanished.**

A LASTING LEGACY

Following Ponce de León's discovery in 1513, the Gulf Stream was first charted on a map by William Gerard de Brahm in 1765. A decade later, Benjamin Franklin wrote about the spectacular blue of the water and persuaded his relative, Timothy Folger, to take its measurements. It proved difficult, however, for ships to remain stable enough in the current's force to permit measuring it. Finally, the American lieutenant John Pillsbury overcame the problem with an ingenious method of anchoring.

Today, special floats bearing transmitters are used to take measurements of the rate of flow of the Gulf Stream, as well as the water's salinity and temperature. Heat-sensitive cameras are used to photograph it from satellites.

DEATH AND DESTRUCTION

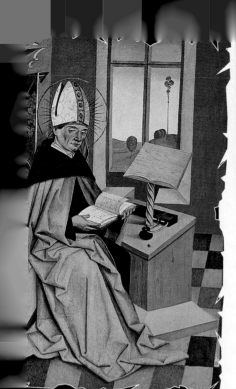

Although Ponce de León died at the hands of Native people, European explorers brought widespread death and destruction to Native peoples throughout the world.

A document called the Requirement was added to a contract between Ponce de León and King Ferdinand, requiring that the Native population of Florida should convert to Christianity. The Requirement also stated that each succeeding pope (the leader of the Roman Catholic Church) had total jurisdiction over the entire world. A bishop (*above*) had supervisory power over priests within the Roman Catholic Church.

Early in 1521, Ponce de León was at long last able to sail to Florida for a second time. He hoped to found a European settlement and take control of the land for Spain. But after less than four months ashore, he and his companions were forced by Native warriors to flee. They sought refuge in the Spanish colony on Cuba. There, Ponce de León died at the age of 47, a few days after being badly wounded in battle against Native warriors in Florida. An arrow gashed his thigh, and his wound probably became infected. It has been speculated that the arrowhead was coated with poison. Native healers, hunters, and warriors all knew how to extract toxic substances from local plants.

EUROPEAN IMPACT

When European explorers and settlers arrived in the New World, they introduced many changes, including previously unknown crops (such as bananas, oranges, and sugarcane), European-style laws, social customs, ways of working, and religious beliefs.

They made these changes for two reasons. One, they felt more comfortable with the familiar lifestyle of their own homelands. Two, they thought that their own religious beliefs and the laws and customs based on them were superior to all others.

For some explorers, especially Hernán Cortés, who conquered the Aztec people of Mexico in 1521, there was another reason — greed for wealth and power.

> 66 *We require that you . . . acknowledge the Church as the Ruler and Superior of the whole world. . . . If you do so . . . their Highnesses will reward you and grant you many benefits.* 99

This carving (*below*) is believed to be a representation of a Native deity.

Not all European explorers, however, were so brutal or excessive. Many, including Ponce de León, wanted the excitement of new experiences. Explorers also intended to build up profitable businesses in the New World, help their country, and advance their families while keeping within the law.

They expected to face some conflict as Native peoples fought to defend their homelands against settlers from overseas. They probably did not, however, intend to bring such widespread death and destruction to the New World.

DEVASTATING EFFECTS

Nevertheless, Europeans had a devastating impact wherever they conquered and settled. This was partly due to the large number of Native people who died from European diseases. Thousands of Native men and women also died in fighting, however. Although

Ponce de León was killed by a Native's arrow, European guns and crossbows were generally much more deadly than Native American war clubs and long bows. Horses (which Ponce de León raised on his farm) also gave settlers an advantage. The horses terrified Native people who had never seen them and did not know what they were. (Horses had become extinct in North and South America thousands of years before.) Horses also allowed European riders to travel much more quickly than Native people who traveled on foot.

Forced labor, capture, and slavery all seriously

In this painting (*right*), St. Peter is seen baptizing a new convert to Christianity. Although the Requirement stated that it was not essential for Natives to change their religion, it nonetheless ordered terrible punishments if they did not join the Christian Church.

Spanish conquistadors tried to convert Native people to Christianity wherever in the world they seized land. In this illustration (*above*), Spanish priests are shown converting Aztec Indians in Mexico.

disrupted Native villages and farms and were a personal disaster for the Native men and women involved.

In the long run, it was the Europeans' religious beliefs that proved most damaging to Native American civilizations. Christian preachers taught Native people that their traditional beliefs were wicked and wrong, and they tried to suppress them. They encouraged Native people to believe that their souls could only be saved through Christianity and claimed that it was essential to destroy Native works of art that had been used in religious ceremonies or that portrayed local gods. Even more damaging, they encouraged European settlers to think that they had a God-given right to rule, in their own way, all non-Christian lands in the New World.

SUCCESS OR FAILURE?

Measured by what he set out to achieve, Juan Ponce de León was a failure. He did not achieve his ambition to conquer Florida for Spain. The first permanent Spanish settlement in Florida was not built until 1565, by Pedro Menéndez de Avilés on the site of present-day St. Augustine. Before this, French explorers had founded the first permanent European settlement in what is now Fort Caroline, South Carolina, in 1564 and had claimed large parts of the nearby coast for France.

Today, however, Juan Ponce de León is remembered for making the first European voyage to explore Bimini, giving Florida a name that has lasted for nearly 500 years, and recognizing the importance of the Gulf Stream.

The exploitation by Spain of Native populations was common throughout the Americas. This 16th-century image (*right*) shows people being captured as slaves in Peru.

For Further Discussion

There are many aspects of Juan Ponce de León's travels that are thought to be controversial and therefore open to debate. The following questions can be used to guide classroom discussion.

1 Do you think that the legendary Fountain of Youth might really exist somewhere in the world?

2 Why did King Ferdinand encourage Ponce de León's voyages to Florida?

3 What caused the bitter rivalry between Diego, son of Christopher Columbus, and Ponce de León?

4 Should the Castilian rulers have given Ponce de León direct financial help for his expeditions?

5 What effect does the Gulf Stream, identified by Ponce de León, continue to have on world climate?

6 Does Ponce de León seem to have been a likeable man? What faults, if any, did he have?

7 Do you think that Ponce de León deserved to be rewarded for services to the monarchy? What rewards would you have given him?

8 Was Ponce de León neglectful in any way to his wife and children?

9 Imagine what might have happened if Ponce de León had not been killed at the age of 47. What do you think he might have gone on to achieve?

10 Did Diego Columbus act fairly toward Ponce de León?

11 What is your opinion of the Requirement? Do you think Ponce de León agreed with the terms of this document?

12 Who do you believe can rightly be called the true discoverer of North America?

13 Do you agree that Ponce de León seems to have excelled as a leader? Why or why not?

14 How was Ponce de León helped during his lifetime and by whom? How was he hindered and by whom?

15 If you were given the task of erecting a new monument to mark the achievements of Juan Ponce de León, where would you place it and what form would you like it to take?

MAJOR WORLD EVENTS

Vasco da Gama (*above*) forced Native people to trade after a battle at Malabar.

During the time that Juan Ponce de León sailed with Columbus, became governor of Puerto Rico, and explored Florida, other Europeans were exploring India, Newfoundland, Peru, Chile, and Venezuela.

Find out about some of these major world events (*right*) and judge how they may have affected Ponce de León's accomplishments.

1497 Sailing from England, John Cabot's ship, the *Matthew*, reached Newfoundland on the eastern seaboard of North America, now a part of Canada.

1497–1498 The Portuguese explorer Vasco da Gama succeeded in establishing the first maritime route to India by sailing around the Cape of Good Hope, Africa.

1499 Alonso de Hojeda and Juan de la Cosa sailed to a place in South America they called *Little Venice*, or "Venezuela."

1499 Italian explorer Amerigo Vespucci reached the Gulf of Venezuela and the mouth of the Amazon River.

1513 Vasco Nuñez de Balboa, a friend of Ponce de León, claimed the Pacific Ocean for Castile.

1519–1521 Portuguese explorer Ferdinand Magellan became the first person to circumnavigate the world.

1532–1535 The Spanish conquistador Francisco Pizarro defeated the Incan Empire in Peru.

1535–1537 Diego de Almagro crossed the Andes mountains and became the first European to reach the land we now know as Chile.

Hernán Cortés, who conquered the Aztecs, is seen here with their King, Montezuma (*below*).

OVER THE YEARS

- A statue of Juan Ponce de León is located in the Plaza de San José in San Juan, Puerto Rico.

After Juan Ponce de León was knighted by King Ferdinand of Castile in 1514, he was always addressed with the title "Don."

- Ponce de León's tomb, in the Cathedral of San Juan, Puerto Rico, is a national monument.

- The city of Ponce on the south coast of Puerto Rico was established in Ponce de León's memory in 1670. Its port, Playa de Ponce, is one of the most important on Puerto Rico.

- A main street in San Juan, Puerto Rico, has become a memorial to this explorer. It is known as the Avenida Ponce de León.

- The Ponce de León Lighthouse, located near Daytona Beach in Volusia County, Florida, is a national landmark. It was designed by Francis Hopkinson Smith and completed in 1883.

- A county and a small town in Florida have been named after Ponce de León.

- Several businesses in Florida have adopted the name of Ponce de León.

- On October 12, 1982, a 29-cent commemorative stamp depicting Ponce de León was issued in Puerto Rico by the U.S. Postal Service.

- There is a statue of Ponce de León in the town of St. Augustine, Florida, but no one is sure if he actually visited this spot.

- A major tourist attraction in St. Augustine, Florida, is called the Fountain of Youth, for the legendary site that Ponce de León wanted to find.

- At Caparra on Puerto Rico, where Ponce de León initially made his home, the ruins of his house have been preserved, and there is a museum there as well.

Widely regarded throughout the United States as one of the most eminent Spanish explorers because of his exploration of Florida, Juan Ponce de León's achievements have been marked in many ways since his death nearly 500 years ago.

Discover how some of his achievements have been remembered (*left*).

GLOSSARY

amulet: a lucky charm believed to protect against evil.

Aztecs: people who founded the Mexican Empire conquered by Spain in 1519.

Bahamas: a group of islands in the Caribbean that was once part of a region known as Bimini.

Bimini: the former name for the area around the Bahamas.

Borinquén: a former name for the island of Puerto Rico.

Christians: people who believe in the teachings of Jesus Christ.

circumnavigate: to go completely around the Earth.

class system: a practice whereby people sharing the same economic and social status are grouped together and do or do not receive privileges because of the group they belong to.

colonize: to create a settlement of people away from their parent government.

conquistadors: Spanish conquerors of the Americas in the 16th century.

convert: to convince people to change from one religion to another.

crest: an identifying emblem.

distorted: twisted or changed, as in a meaning that is no longer completely true.

Dominican Republic: the easternmost nation on the island of Hispaniola.

Don: used as a prefix before a Spanish nobleman's name. Similar to "Sir."

economic: relating to the production, distribution, and consumption of goods and services.

Española: another name for Hispaniola.

eternal: everlasting or never ending.

foot soldier: a soldier trained and armed to fight on foot.

friar: a man belonging to a certain Christian religious order.

Gulf Stream: a warm current in the Atlantic Ocean that flows from the Gulf of Mexico northeast along the U.S. coast to Europe.

Haiti: the westernmost nation on the island of Hispaniola.

Higüey: a district in what is now known as the Dominican Republic.

Hispaniola: an island in the Caribbean Sea now divided into Haiti and the Dominican Republic.

Incan: pertaining to the people of Peru who had an empire until the Spanish conquest.

Jewish: relating to the people who believe in the religion of Judaism.

maritime: pertaining to the sea.

measles: a contagious disease that shows as red circular spots on the skin.

missionaries: people who set out to convert others to their own religion.

monastery: a residence for monks — men who are members of a certain religious order.

Muslims: people who follow the teachings of Muhammad and the faith of Islam.

noble: a person or people born into privilege.

page: a boy who acts as an assistant or who will be trained as a knight.

pope: the head of the Catholic Church.

province: a region of a country.

Puerto Rico: the island formerly known as San Juan Bautista and Borinquén.

Requirement: a document added to a contract between Ponce de León and King Ferdinand, requiring that the Native population of Florida should convert to Christianity.

Roman Catholic Church: a Christian church headed by the Pope.

salinity: the amount of salt contained in something.

San Juan Bautista: a former name for the island of Puerto Rico.

shrewd: possessing a sharp awareness or clever understanding.

sirens: part-human, female creatures in Greek mythology who lured men to destruction with their singing.

smallpox: a contagious disease whereby blisterlike eruptions form on the skin and cause severe scarring.

sponsored: being supported by another with money or in another way in order to complete a project or activity.

submersible: a craft able to go underwater.

thermal: involving the heat or temperature of something.

Tropic of Cancer: the parallel of latitude that is 23.5 degrees north of the equator.

FOR FURTHER STUDY

BOOKS

Juan Ponce de León. Sean Dolan
(Chelsea House Publishers)

Juan Ponce de León. Ruth Manning
(Heinemann Library)

Juan Ponce de León. Gail Sakurai
(Franklin Watts)

**Juan Ponce de León: And the Search
for the Fountain of Youth.** Dan Harmon
(Chelsea House Publishers)

**Juan Ponce de León and the Spanish
Discovery of Puerto Rico and Florida.**
Robert H. Fuson (McDonald & Woodward
Publishing Company)

Ponce de León. Wyatt Blassingame
(Chelsea House Publishers)

Ponce de León. Trish Kline (Rourke Book
Company)

**Ponce de León and the Discovery of
Florida: The Man, the Myth, and the Truth.**
Douglas T. Peck (Pogo Press)

**Ponce de León: Juan Ponce de León
Searches for the Fountain of Youth.**
Ann Heinrichs (Compass Point Books)

Travels of Juan Ponce de León.
Deborah Crisfield (Raintree Steck-Vaughn)

VIDEOS

American Tall Tales: Ponce de León.
(Lyrick Studios Video)

Biography: Ponce de León.
(A&E Entertainment)

WEB SITES

Find a Grave.
**www.findagrave.com/cgi-bin/fg.cgi?page=
gr&GRid=825**

Floridians Conquistadors.
**www.floridahistory.org/floridians/conquis.
htm**

Juan Ponce de León: Explorer.
**www.enchantedlearning.com/explorers/
page/d/deleon.shtml**

Ponce de León.
**multimedia.esuhsd.org/2000/ed_project/
135_web/studentprojects/ageexploration/
poncedeleon.html**

Ponce de León, Juan.
**www.infoplease.com/ce6/people/
A0839647.html**

Their Stamp on History.
**www.stamponhistory.com/people/
deleon.html**

Who Was Ponce de León?
**www.publicbookshelf.com/public_html/
Our_Country_Vol_1/whowaspo_bf.html**